The Three R's:
Reuse, reduce, recycle

Núria Roca

Illustrations: **Rosa M. Curto**

BARRON'S

Do you know the letter **R?** It is the first letter in three words that teach us different ways to fight pollution. It is the **R** in Reuse, Reduce, and Recycle. Do you know these words **?**

Reuse things that are still in good shape, such as your big brother's jacket.

Reduce the amount of things we throw away, such as paper cups.

Recycle old things to make new ones, such as a puppet out of an old sock!

In the town where Paul lives, people throw their garbage bags into a garbage container at the corner. In the morning, a garbage truck empties the container and takes the garbage bags… do you know where?
To a garbage **landfill** or **dump**, which is a huge place in the mountains or in the countryside, far from the city.

In Paul's town, however, there are so many people and so much garbage is produced that every landfill is full already, and nobody knows where to build another. So they have built a huge furnace called an **incinerator** to burn all the waste material.

Nobody likes to live close by; people think the smoke coming out of the chimney is harmful to plants, animals, and people.

At Paul's school they have talked about the huge amount of **waste** produced in just one day, and they have decided to reuse as many things as they can. That means that now they will use every object many times, until it breaks or cannot be used anymore.

At his school, they paint both sides of all sheets of paper, use the empty cans of paint to keep paper clips and rubber bands, and use the pieces of paper left over to make wonderful collages. Do **you** have any other ideas?

At home, everybody reuses as many things as possible. Paul wears the T-shirts that his big brother has outgrown and also plays with many of his old toys. Can you guess how many objects on the right page may be used **over** and **over?**

Paul's brother outgrew his bike and now Paul rides it, and since he has no use for his tricycle anymore, he has passed it on to his cousin.

Something else we do at home and at school is trying not to waste **water** or **electricity,** because this way we help take care of our planet. It seems very little, but the drops of water from a leaking faucet could fill up a bathtub in a day!

So keep the water and lights off—when they are not needed, of course!

When Paul and his family go **shopping** for food, they take their own baskets or bags made of cloth. By doing that, they won't have to ask for plastic or paper bags at the super-market and will reduce the amount of plastic and paper made by factories. Reducing means **using** very **little,** only what is needed.

Plastic bags are very handy, but sometimes they end up in the sea, where they can be **dangerous** for animals. Turtles may take them for jellyfish and eat them, or they may get tangled up in the plastic rings used to hold cans together.
It is very important not to litter the ground, the woods, the beach, the ocean, or the city!

Paper
paste

Wet
paper

Press

Drying machine

Calender for smoothing

18

At Paul's school they throw all paper and cardboard into
a special street container. Then trucks pick up everything
and take it to a paper mill, where used paper and
cardboard is shredded and washed until it becomes
a pulp that is wet and soft.
With this pulp they **make** paper **again.**
When it gets dry, we have… recycled paper!

Practically everything can be recycled: paper and cardboard, plastic objects, glass, cans… All these things are first shredded, ground, or pulped, and then they go through different processes that make **new** drinking cans, glass bottles, plastic containers…

At school we make paper paste out of torn and wet old papers.

Old papers

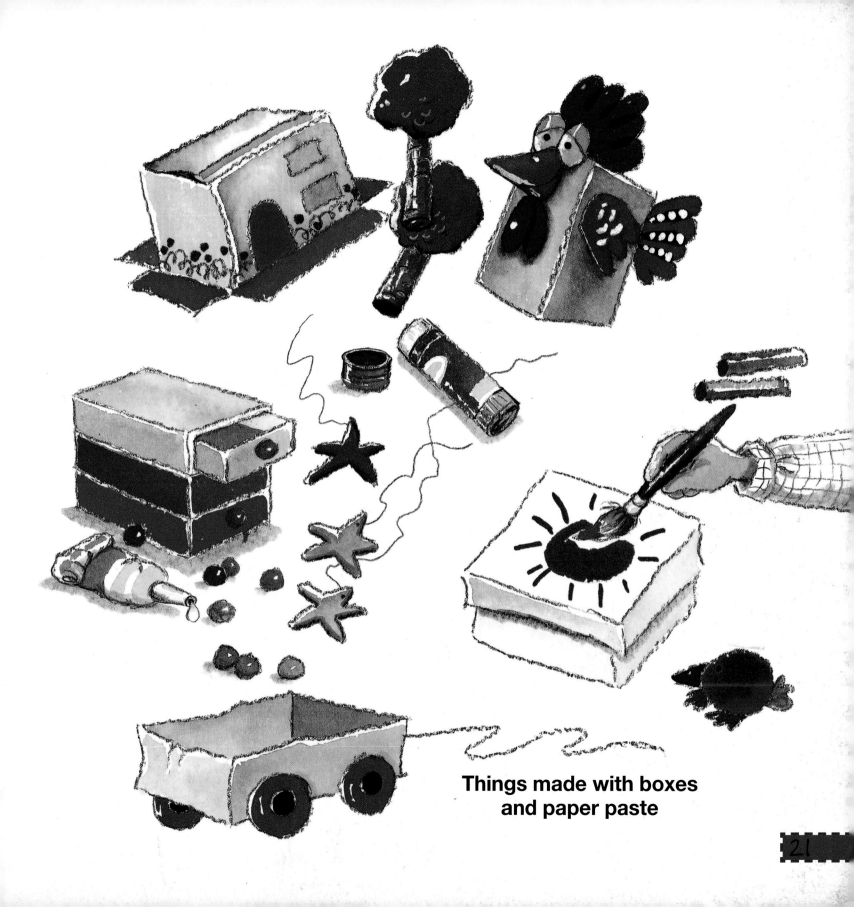

Things made with boxes and paper paste

Paul's parents have told him that food scraps can also be recycled. All food that otherwise would be wasted can be made into fertilizer, which is food for plants. The fertilizer produced this way is called **compost.** The banana peels and lemon rinds Paul has just thrown into the garbage may become food for plants, like all food scraps. That's **great!**

What can be recycled?

But if we want to recycle, we have to put the waste in special **containers.** Now, in the kitchen at Paul's home there is a container for things made of plastic, metal or glass, and another for all the other garbage. Also, all newspapers and magazines are neatly tied in packages so that they also can be recycled.

At some schools they also collect used batteries. The children have been told batteries may not be recycled and that they pollute a lot, so it is very important not to throw them in the garbage. That's why the children have made a special container for them.

Once it is full, they will take it to a **recycling center,** where the metal from the batteries will be used to make new ones.

The drawings to decorate the container are the work of Paul's class. Nice job, isn't it?

If we waste less and recycle all we can, there will be less pollution and we will be able to **live** for a long time in our little planet, breathing smokeless air, swimming in clear waters, and strolling through woods and countryside free from garbage.

Paul thinks it is worth the effort. How about **you?**

A birdhouse

Using recycled materials you can build a birdhouse like this one. You just need:
• An empty milk or orange juice carton
• A pair of scissors
• About seven feet of string
• Water-resistant adhesive tape
and the help of a grownup!

1. Cut off the top of the container, rinse it well, and make a round hole on one of the sides as shown in the drawing.
2. On the opposite side of the pack make two small holes to pass the string through. Tie a couple of knots on the inside of the pack so the string will remain in place.

3. Make a bed for the birds by placing dry grass on the bottom of the box. Then close the top of the pack with the lid and use some adhesive tape so the rain will not leak inside.

Now you just have to look for a tree in your garden or at a friend's garden and tie the strings hanging from the box around a branch or the tree trunk.

It's only a question of time before a bird decides to go into its new house!

Stale-bread pudding

Paul loves a pudding his dad makes when they have bread left over. Would you like to taste it? You only need:

- 2 glasses of hot milk
- 4 thin slices of bread without crust
- 10 spoonfuls of sugar and 4 spoonfuls of water
- 3 eggs
- 4 spoonfuls of orange marmalade
- 2 spoonfuls of raisins

AND THE HELP FROM YOUR PARENTS!

1. Crumb the bread into a bowl, add the hot milk and let the bread soak in it until it is very soft.

2. Put the 4 spoonfuls of water and 4 spoonfuls of sugar in a microwave-safe rectangular pan. Microwave it for 6 minutes, and you will see that the water and the sugar become caramel. Move the pan so the sides are coated with caramel.

3. When the bread is soft, add the eggs, the remaining sugar, and the marmalade. Blend all these ingredients well and pour them into the caramelized pan.

4. Microwave between 10–12 minutes. Stick a fork in it to see if it is done and, if it is cooked, you may take it out of the pan.

You have recycled bread and now you have a delicious pudding!

An experiment

Food soon disappears; plastic and aluminum do not

1. Ask your parents to give you a tomato that is overripe or any fruit that no longer is fit to eat.

2. Find a plastic bottle and a piece of used aluminum foil.

3. Put the three things separately, in a place where it is wet and shady (a flowerpot in the balcony, or a corner of the garden).

4. Watch them everyday to see what happens.

See how the tomato or the fruit gets spots all over? They look like spots but actually they are fungi, like the mushrooms we may find in the woods, only so tiny you would need a very strong magnifying glass to be able to see them. That's what happens in the woods with food or pieces of plants and animals: very tiny fungi and bugs eat everything up and make it disappear in a few days. Aluminum foil and plastic, however, do not spoil or rot, that's why it is so important not to leave them in the woods, the seashore, or the countryside. Anything you throw away made of glass, plastic, or metal will stay there for many long years, polluting everything and hurting animals and plants.

Let's make a notebook

We can use sheets of paper with only one side used, like defective sheets from the printer or the photocopier at school or at home.

1. Collect all sheets of paper you find that have an unused side (ten sheets are enough).

2. Place them one on top of the other in perfect order.

3. Fold the group of sheets in half and then unfold it.

4. Make two holes right in the middle of the folding line.

5. Thread a thick string that is about two feet long and tie a knot. Don't cut the remaining string: you may use it to bind the notebook so it will stay closed.

If you recycle paper, there will less need to make paper. This way you help to save trees, because paper is made from trees. Did you know that?

How about drawing a big R on the front page? The R for RECYCLED!

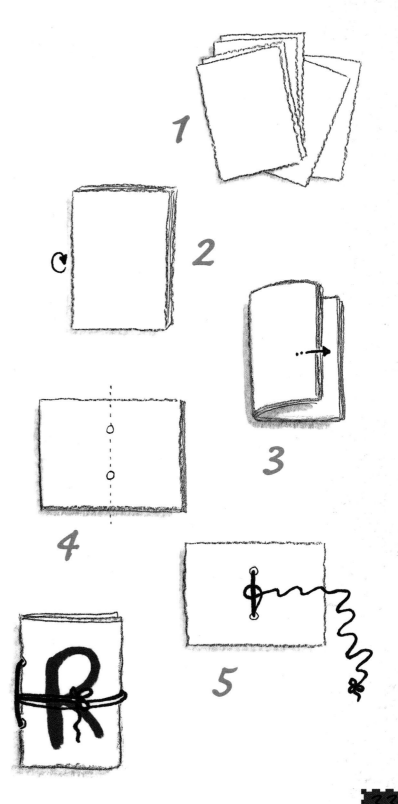

Note to parents

We humans use a lot of raw materials and energy to produce a great quantity of objects: pencils, cars, tables, toys… However, we often neglect the fact that these resources may be depleted, that extracting these materials from the environment where they are found may cause serious environmental impact, and that unrestrained consumption produces incredibly big amounts of garbage.

Garbage: a problem

Most waste material produced at home is burned or buried. Modern dumps or landfills are controlled, meaning that they are lined in the inside so the refuse and the ooze coming out of it will not be in contact with the ground. When the garbage trucks dump the refuse into the landfill, a steamroller crushes the garbage and afterwards a layer of earth is spread on top. When the landfill is full, all its surface is covered with soil and a lawn may be planted on top. This way the dump may become a park. When the dump site is filled up, we need to find another place to keep burying the garbage.

The scarcity of such places makes it necessary to burn the refuse in special plants called incinerators, which are very expensive to build and maintain. Even if there are laws regulating gas emissions so they do not exceed hazardous limits for people, these incinerators still produce polluting gases, as well as ashes that are toxic for our health and that must be buried or stored somewhere.

To reduce the amount of trash and energy consumption, we should reduce the amount of throwaway things we buy; we may also reuse things as many times as possible before throwing them away, and we should recycle objects such as glass jars and bottles to make other useful products from them. Ultimately, it is a question of implementing the three R's: reduce, reuse, and recycle. And the best time to start is at an early age.

The 3 R's

To Reduce means to throw away less, and one of the best ways to do this is to refrain from buying what we really do not need.

To Reuse means keeping something and using it again. We can stop many things ending up in the dump, such as a book, a jacket, or a bike, by using them again or giving them out to somebody who may have a use for them.

To Recycle means processing used materials to produce new objects. Aluminum soda cans, glass bottles, paper and cardboard, and plastic containers may be taken to recycling centers where these used objects are classified and sent to factories to be made into new products. Old papers are converted into paper pulp, from which new paper is made. Glass bottles are crushed and melted to make new glass products. Aluminum cans are melted and made into aluminium sheets used for new cans or other aluminum products. The target is to create a new product from a used one.

Things you and your family can do

- Save energy (water, electricity, gasoline)
- Separate recyclable materials: paper, glass, plastic, metal
- Avoid using spray cans
- Use public transport, ride bicycles, or walk
- Avoid appliances run by batteries and, if you use them, do not throw the batteries in the garbage
- Open the windows for airing when heating/air conditioning is off. We should do this at the least cold moment of the day in winter and the least hot moment of the day in summer
- Set the thermostat at a reasonable temperature (between 65°F and 69° F)
- Turn off the light when it is not needed
- Turn off the faucet while you brush your teeth to save water
- Use biodegradable detergents and cleansers

THE THREE R'S: REUSE, REDUCE, RECYCLE

First edition for the United States and Canada published
in 2007 by Barron's Educational Series, Inc.
© Copyright 2006 by Gemser Publications S.L.
C/Castell, 38; Teià (08329) Barcelona, Spain. (World Rights)

Author: **Núria Roca**
Illustrator: **Rosa M. Curto**

All inquiries should be addressed to:
Barron's Educational Series, Inc.
250 Wireless Boulevard
Hauppauge, NY 11788
http://www.barronseduc.com

ISBN-13: 978-0-7641-3581-1
ISBN-10: 0-7641-3581-3
Library of Congress Control Number 2006931048

Printed in China
9 8 7 6 5 4 3 2 1